John Lawson Stoddard

Egypt

John Lawson Stoddard

Egypt

ISBN/EAN: 9783337325565

Printed in Europe, USA, Canada, Australia, Japan

Cover: Foto ©Andreas Hilbeck / pixelio.de

More available books at **www.hansebooks.com**

EGYPT

BY

JOHN L. STODDARD

ILLUSTRATED AND EMBELLISHED WITH ONE HUNDRED
AND NINETEEN REPRODUCTIONS OF
PHOTOGRAPHS

CHICAGO
BELFORD, MIDDLEBROOK & COMPANY
MDCCCXCVII

EGYPT

EGYPT

L ANDS that have made or witnessed history possess peculiar fascination; and when to their historical qualities are added those of the mysterious and the beautiful, their charm is boundless, for then they touch the realm of the imagination, that is to say, the infinite.

Egypt in these respects is unsurpassed. Historically, she is the eldest born of Time; the mother of all subsequent civilizations; the longest lived among the nations of the earth; the teacher of art, philosophy, and religion before Greece and Rome were born. When everywhere else rude huts and primitive tents were mankind's highest forms of

AN EGYPTIAN LANDSCAPE.

architecture, Egypt was rearing her stupendous pyramids and temples, which still remain the marvel of the world.

It stirs the blood merely to read the names of the great actors in that mighty drama of the past, whose theatre was

the valley of the Nile. For Egypt is the land of Rameses
and the Pharaohs; of Joseph and of Moses; of Alexander
the Great and the Ptolemies; of Cæsar, Antony, and Cleopatra,—a land beside whose awful ruins the Colosseum of

HARBOR OF ALEXANDRIA.

Rome, the Parthenon of Athens, and even the Temple of
Jerusalem, are the productions of yesterday.

But Egypt is also a land of mystery. Her history goes
back so far that it is finally lost in the unknown, as the Nile
Valley gradually gives place to the sands of the Sahara. Her
very origin appears at first miraculous. For Egypt has been
literally built up by that mysterious river whose sources have,
till recently, perplexed and baffled all explorers for five thousand years. Her situation also is unique,—a palm-girt path
of civilization walled in by two deserts. Silence broods over
her. Solemnity environs her. She is a land in which the
dead alone are great:—a temple of antiquity, whose monuments are the eternal Pyramids and Sphinx. Her glory is
secure beyond the possibility of loss, embalmed in art and
literature like her mummied kings.

What wonder, then, that standing on the shadowy
threshold of prehistoric times, Egypt still charms us by the
irresistible attraction of undying fame? What marvel that
her vast antiquity and changeless calm possess a power, like
that of fabled Lethe, to render us forgetful of the feverish
excitements of the western world, and from her silent and enduring monuments to teach us the littleness of gods and men?

Alexandria is the front door of Egypt, as Suez, on the
Red Sea, is its portal from the rear. Through this historic

CÆSAR AND CLEOPATRA.

city of the Mediterranean the tide of Occidental travel every
winter ebbs and flows as surely as the rise and fall of the
majestic Nile. Unlike the rest of Egypt, however, Alexandria lacks the flavor of remote antiquity. A century ago

a traveler said of it that it resembled an orphan child, who had inherited from his father nothing but his name. Hence it is hard to realize, when one stands within its walls to-day, that twenty centuries ago Alexandria ranked among the largest and most brilliant cities in the world, and was the principal emporium of the East, receiving the products of interior Africa, Arabia, and India, and forwarding them to all other sections of the Roman empire, till the astonished Cæsars half believed the assertion that the Alexandrians possessed the power of making gold. This city was, moreover, for centuries the principal seat of Grecian learning; and here St. Mark is said to have proclaimed the Gospel, with the result that Alexandria finally became the intellectual stronghold of Christianity.

CLEOPATRA'S NEEDLE.

Nor can the tourist forget that this was the favorite city of two conquerors, unrivaled in their way,—the first, its earliest ruler, Alexander; the second, its last queen, the peerless Cleopatra. One subdued empires; the other conquered hearts; for who can think of Alexandria without recalling how the "Enchantress of the Nile" here captivated the world's conqueror, Julius Cæsar, and subsequently made the great Triumvir, Antony, her willing slave for fourteen years?

But war and pillage have destroyed the relics of old Alexandria almost as completely as though a tidal wave from the adjoining ocean had swept over it. Its pure white marble lighthouse, Pharos, which surpassed the Pyramids in height, and was considered one of the seven wonders of the world, is now no longer visible. The mausoleum of Alexander the Great, in which the youthful conqueror's body lay in a sarcophagus of pure gold, has also passed away. The immense Alexandrian library,—the largest of antiquity,—has long since vanished in flame and smoke.

The magnificent Museum of Ptolemy Philadelphus, which,

APPROACH TO POMPEY'S PILLAR.

two and a half centuries before Christ, was the acknowledged meeting-place of scholars and sages from all lands, and the focus of the intellectual life of the world, has so effectually disappeared that no one can determine with certainty its ancient site. Even in modern times Alexandria has suffered spoliation. Until quite recently, the traveler saw upon its shore—one prostrate, one erect—the obelisks known as Cleopatra's Needles, which were hewn from the quarry thirty-five hundred years ago. But these have been conveyed to distant lands,—one of them standing now beside the Thames in London, the other in Central Park, New York. From the earliest times the obelisks of Egypt have fascinated travelers. The Assyrians and Persians carried some of them away. Rome has eleven in her streets to-day. Another stands in Constantinople; while, beside the Seine, the obelisk of Luxor rebukes with its solemnity the whirl of gaiety in the modern capital of pleasure. Only one great memorial of the past remains in Alexandria. It is the stately monolith of red granite, misnamed Pompey's Pillar.

For ages it was supposed that this imposing shaft, which with its capital and pedestal attains a height of more than a hundred feet, had been erected here in memory of Cæsar's mighty rival, who, fleeing southward after the battle of Pharsalia, was murdered on the Egyptian coast. But the name Pompeius, sculptured on its pedestal, is merely that of the Roman prefect who reared this magnificent column to the Roman emperor Diocletian, in the third century after Christ, perhaps in gratitude for a gift of grain that he had sent to Alexandria. The statue which adorned its summit long since disappeared, leaving no trace behind to tell us whom it represented; and whether or not this noble

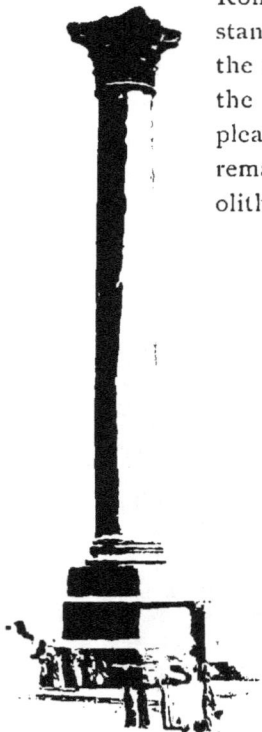

POMPEY'S PILLAR.

column once formed part of an Egyptian temple founded long anterior to the Romans, is still a matter of dispute. Beyond all question, however, is the fact that its shadow falls to-day upon a dreary Arab cemetery,—pathetic symbol of the buried glories of the city it once adorned.

SUEZ CANAL.

The European quarter of Alexandria is well lighted and possesses many handsome residences. Much capital is invested here, and evidences of wealth abound. The future prosperity of the city seems assured. Within its sheltered harbor is abundant sea-room for the largest fleets, and from this ocean gateway railroads now extend to Cairo, Port Saïd, Suez, and the Upper Nile; while at this point the Mediterranean cable joins the telegraph wire along whose metal

HOTEL ABBAT, ALEXANDRIA.

thread the messages of war and commerce, or tender words of love to distant friends, may be conveyed at lightning speed from Europe, Asia, or America, to the heart of Africa.

The main business section of Alexandria is the Square of Mehemet Ali. Fronting on this long rectangle are the principal hotels, banks, and steamship offices, and in the centre is the equestrian statue of the first Viceroy of Egypt, whose name the area bears. One would expect to see his statue

here, for Mehemet Ali was the most remarkable man the Orient has produced in the last
hundred years. His influence is felt here to

this day. Without him Egypt could
not have attained her present position
of semi-independence and prosperity.
For forty years he was the arbiter of
Egypt. He was a despot; but there
are times when autocratic sovereigns
are a necessity. Nations are like in-
dividuals: at certain stages in their
history they need authority and disci-
pline to force them into habits of in-
dustry and unquestioning obedience.
Alexandria has reason to be grateful to

AN EGYPTIAN PORTER.

Mehemet Ali. Before he made himself dictator of Egypt,
and freed himself from vassalage to the Sultan, the splendid
city of the Ptolemies had dwindled into insignificance, and was

a mere haunt of
fishermen and
pirates. But in
a dozen years
he transformed
it, until it was
once more an
entrepôt of
Eastern trade, a
half-way house
to India, and
the great meet-
ing point of
Europe, Africa,
and Asia. At
his command its

A PALACE OF THE KHEDIVE.

harbor was reopened and made safe for merchant ships, and his indomitable energy soon caused a huge canal to be constructed, which proved to be one of the most important works of modern times,—a navigable waterway by which the traffic of the Nile was brought to Alexandria. This Mahmoodiah Canal was made within the space of a year. A quarter of a million natives were compelled to labor on it, and of these twenty-five thousand are said to have perished on its banks

SQUARE OF MEHEMET ALI.

from overwork and insufficient food. But, while lamenting the cruelty attending its construction, we must concede to the Egyptian autocrat full credit for the work achieved, which has raised Alexandria from poverty, and filled its empty treasury with constantly increasing wealth. Mehemet Ali, like most great geniuses, was a "self-made man," rising by his undoubted talents from the position of a colonel in the Turkish army to be Viceroy of Egypt and the founder of the present dynasty.

He was a proof of how the Orient, once so prolific of
great men, can still surprise us.   Give to the East a leader
capable of arousing its enthusiasm and of kindling its relig-
ious zeal, and Europe might again be forced to struggle
desperately for its life and liberties.   Thus, coming like a
thunderbolt from a clear sky, Mehemet Ali, with twenty-
four thousand men, emerged from Egypt, conquered Syria,

CAIRO.

and drove the Turks before him into the heart of Asia
Minor.   Under the leadership of Mehemet's dashing son,
Ibrahim (a son worthy of such a father), the Egyptians
fought as they had never fought before.   Mehemet Ali was
declared an outlaw; but army after army sent against him
by the Sultan was hopelessly defeated.   The victor rapidly
approached the Bosporus; Constantinople itself seemed actually within his grasp; but the united powers of Europe,
startled by this sudden resurrection of the Orient, cried in

the thunder of a hundred cannon, "Halt!" and Ibrahim could go no farther. Baffled and broken-hearted, the great adventurer returned with his son to Egypt, the sovereignty of which he still retained, and to console himself for the failure of his brilliant dream of Eastern conquest and extensive empire, he gained at least the privilege of bequeathing to his descendants his viceregal power.

AN EGYPTIAN PEASANT.

But, interesting as one may at first find the cosmopolitan and progressive city of Alexandria, it is by no means thoroughly Egyptian, and should be regarded as merely a door-

VEGETATION IN THE DELTA.

way to the real glories of the land of the Pharaohs.   Hence, after a stay of a few days on the coast, one always hastens into the interior of the country.

A bird's-eye view of Lower Egypt would reveal a vast expanse of cultivated territory in the form of a triangle, the base of which is on the Mediterranean.   From its resemblance to the fourth letter of the Greek alphabet, this area has for ages been appropriately called the Delta.   A poet has compared it to a beautiful green fan, with Cairo sparkling like a diamond in its handle.

THE MENA HOTEL.

The simile is an apt one, for in the days of the Caliphs, a thousand years ago, Cairo was the brightest jewel of the Nile,—the rival of Bagdad and Damascus in the annals of the Arabian Nights; and even now, to one who comes to it directly from the Occident, its Oriental brilliancy is most impressive.

On my first visit to Egypt in the days of Ismail Pasha, there was practically only one Cairo.   Now there are two,— the African and European,—contending, not for political supremacy, which has been definitely won by England, but for supremacy in architecture, dress, and manners.

A MARKET NEAR CAIRO.

New Cairo has become a charming winter residence, but the old city of the Caliphs, as the traveler saw it only thirty years ago, is gone. Red-coated British soldiers now swarm upon the citadel of Mehemet Ali; Egyptian troops wear European uniforms; the narrow, covered streets, which painters like Gérôme so loved to reproduce, have largely given place to broad, unshadowed thoroughfares; and most of the exquisitely carved and inlaid balconies which formerly adorned the front of nearly every Cairene house, have disappeared. On the other hand, magnificent hotels have sprung into existence, and in the winter shelter crowds of foreign guests whose ancestors were savages

AN OLD STREET.

for three thousand years after the completion of the Sphinx. One of these hotels has even dared to plant itself at the very base of the Great Pyramid!

Cairo, modernized by the English, may be compared to a fashionable piece of western furniture placed on an eastern rug, or to a Bedouin of the desert wearing a silk hat and a Prince Albert coat. While the city has greatly gained in modern characteristics, as well as in sanitary conditions, it

has lost much of its old picturesqueness. Nevertheless, within
its ancient precincts there are still many streets of Moorish
aspect, with mosques, bazaars, and Oriental dwellings, among
which one seems to be a thousand miles removed from

A LATTICED WINDOW.

western civiliza-
tion. But these
attractive feat-
ures of the past
are undergoing
radical trans-
formation. Dur-
ing the reign of
Ismail Pasha,the
ratio between
the East and
West in Cairo
left little to be
desired, and the
Egyptian capital
then combined
just enough
modern luxuries
and comforts to
offset gracefully some less agreeable characteristics of the
Orient. Thus, even as early as 1871, the Khedive had built
a handsome Opera House in Cairo, and had offered the com-
poser Verdi a munificent sum for an opera which should
represent the glories of old Egypt. The result was that
finest production of the modern Italian school, Aïda, whose
representation here on a scale of great magnificence, with
Madame Parepa Rosa in the title rôle, is one of my most
treasured memories of a winter on the Nile.

Occasionally, in some old, narrow street, one may see,
even now, what was a score of years ago a well-nigh uni-

versal architectural feature of the city, the Mashrebeeyeh, — a latticed window made of cedar wood, inlaid with mother-of-pearl. Such windows are admirably suited to the Orient, for they exclude both light and heat, and also screen the inmates from all observation,—an important consideration in Cairo, since in these narrow passageways, when once above the lower story, the houses rapidly approach each other till their projecting windows almost meet. If you glance up at these, you may perhaps perceive at one of the interstices the flash of a jewel, or the gleam of a bright eye, and hear a musical laugh, or the exclamation, "Giaour!" (Infidel).

MINARETS IN CAIRO.

A stay of only a few hours in Cairo will convince the tourist that the typical animal of Egypt is the donkey. Of these there are said to be fifty thousand in Cairo alone. Most of them are of the color of Maltese

cats, and all are closely clipped, and have their bodies fan-
tastically painted, starred, or striped, until they look like miniature zebras.   They are so small that the feet of their riders

A CAIRENE SIGHT.

almost touch
the ground.
But they are
swift-footed
and easy, and
riding on their
backs is almost
as comfortable
as sitting in a
rocking-chair.
Why has the
donkey never
found a eulo-
gist? The horse
is universally
admired.   The
Arab poet sings
of the beauties
of his camel.

The bull and cow have been held sacred, and even the dog
and cat have been praised in prose and verse.   But the poor
donkey still remains the butt of ridicule, the symbol of stu-
pidity and the object of abuse.   But if there is another and
a better world for animals, and if in that sphere patience ranks
as a prime virtue, the ass will have a better pasture-ground
than many of its rivals.   The donkey's small size exposes it
to cruelty.   When animals have power to defend themselves,
man's caution makes him kinder.   He hesitates to hurt an
elephant, and even respects to some extent the heels of a
mule.   But the donkey corresponds to the small boy who
cannot protect himself in a crowd of brutal playmates.   The

only violent thing about it is its voice, and on the human
ass this voice has very little restraining influence. It is difficult to see how these useful animals could be replaced in
certain countries of the world. Purchased cheaply, reared
inexpensively, living on thistles, if they get nothing better,
and patiently carrying heavy burdens until they drop from
weakness,—these little beasts are of incalculable value to the
laboring classes of Southern Europe, Egypt, Mexico, and
similarly situated lands. If they have failed to win affection,
it is perhaps because of their one infirmity,— the startling
tones which they produce.

On the morning after our arrival in Cairo, we went out
on the steps of Shep-
heard's Hotel prepared
to take a ride through
the city. Directly oppo-
site were thirty
or forty Egyp-
tian donkeys, all
saddled and bri-
dled, awaiting
riders. Their
drivers (whose
principal gar-
ment was a
long woolen
shirt) stood by
them, almost
as anxious to be
employed as
New York hack-

A PROMENADE.

men, for, if they return to their masters at night empty-
handed, they receive a beating. The sight of strangers descending the hotel steps was, therefore, a signal for them

to make a grand rush for-
ward, pushing and crowd-
ing their wretched beasts,
and shouting at the top of
their voices the
ludicrous names
which previous
travelers had be-
stowed upon
these animals: —
"Take mine, good
donkey, — very
good!" "Take
mine, 'Champagne
Charley!'" "Take

SLEEPING DONKEY BOY.

mine, 'Abe Lincoln!'" "Take mine, 'Prince Bismarck!'"
"Take mine, 'Yankee Doodle!'" The noise and confusion
are most comical to an observer. When the stranger has
once mounted,
the boy catches
hold of the don-
key's tail (which
he uses as a rud-
der), gives him a
whack in the rear,
shouts "Ah-ye!
Reglah!" and off
they go, present-
ing a scene that
never failed to
excite our merri-
ment.

AN EGYPTIAN DONKEY.

Towering far
above the city of

the Caliphs is a huge fortress called the Citadel. As is well
known, Cairo is of Arabian origin,—a brilliant memento of
Mohammedan conquest. Its name (in Arabic, Al Kahireh)
signifies "The Victorious." When, in the seventh century after
Christ, the followers of the Prophet, inspired with enthusiasm
for their new   religion, rushed
northward   from Arabia
on their   path of

THE CITADEL.

victory and proselytism (which ultimately made the greater
part of the Mediterranean a Moslem lake), Egypt was one of
their first and most important conquests. Memphis, the ancient City of the Pharaohs, was then still extant, adorned
with many imposing monuments that had survived the lapse
of centuries. But this old capital of an alien faith ill suited

the impetuous zealots of Mohammed. They therefore founded Cairo, only a few miles away, and did not scruple to remove thither, for the construction of its buildings, the blocks of stone of which the palaces and temples of old Memphis were composed. It was the famous Saladin,—the brave and chivalrous foe of Richard the Lion-Hearted in Syria,—who built the citadel of Cairo; and the unscrupulous architect employed by him for this purpose destroyed several small

THE CASTLE OF THE NILE.

pyramids, and used the larger ones, which had been reared five thousand years before, as stone quarries from which to extract building material for this fortress, called by the Arabs the "Castle of the Nile." Here Saladin's successors lived for centuries, making this City of the Caliphs the rival of Damascus; and here, in the present century, the cunning Viceroy, Mehemet Ali, used to sit, like a spider in its web, ready to let loose upon the city below a volley of destruction at the first whisper of revolt. It was here also that, in 1811, this relentless ruler caused his political enemies, the Mamelukes, to be massacred. The name Mameluke signifies "White Slave," and the actual founders of this corps were originally Circassian slaves, who gradually climbed to the position, first of favorites, then of tyrants. It is true, they had helped

Mehemet Ali to secure his place of power;
but he suspected that they regretted it and
were conspiring to destroy him.   At all
events, the Viceroy, having used them as
a ladder for his vast ambition, found it ex-
pedient to get rid of them, as Napoleon, at
the Battle of the Pyramids, had sought to
exterminate them.   Accordingly he invited
these powerful foes to a banquet in the citadel.   They came without suspicion,— four
hundred and eighty in number, superbly
dressed and finely mounted.   But no sooner
had the portals closed behind them, than a
scathing fire was opened upon them by Mehemet Ali's troops, who suddenly appeared
upon the walls.   Unable alike to defend
themselves or to escape, the Mamelukes

AN EGYPTIAN SOLDIER.

fell beneath repeated volleys, horses and men in horrible
confusion, anguish, and despair,—with the exception of one
man, who, spurring his horse in desperation over the welter-
ing bodies of his comrades, forced him to leap over the lofty
parapet.   A shower of bullets followed him, scarcely more
swift than his descending steed, but he escaped as if by
miracle, and freeing himself from his mangled horse, he fled
in safety into the adjoining desert.

VIEW FROM THE CITADEL.

Meantime, in an adjoining room (still shown to visitors), Mehemet Ali is said to have remained, calm and motionless, save for a nervous twitching of his hands, though he could plainly hear the rattle of musketry and the shrieks and groans of the dying.

When all was over, his Italian physician ventured into his presence to congratulate him.   The Viceroy made no reply, but merely asked for drink, and, in a silence more eloquent than any speech, drank a long, deep draught.   He knew that thenceforth he was absolute master of Egypt,—possibly sovereign of the East.

The view at sunset from this Cairene citadel is wonderfully impressive, and during several sojourns in Cairo I rarely failed to climb the hill each evening to enjoy it.   Standing on the parapet of this Arabian fortress, one sees below him

THE DESERT.

in the immediate foreground a grove of graceful minarets, rising like sculptured palm-trees from an undulating mass of foliage and bulbous domes. Beyond these, stretching to the north and south as far as the eye can follow it, is a magnificent belt of verdure.   Along its centre, like a broad band of silver, gleams the river Nile, within whose depths the beautiful Antinous found death for his imperial master, and which at this

point has borne upon its breast the cradle of the infant Moses
and the regal barge of Cleopatra.

Still farther westward, the declining sun seems to be sinking into a violet sea, so mar-
velous is the light that glorifies
the tawny desert,—symbol of
perpetual desolation.   Upon
the edge of that vast area, into
whose depths the orb of day
seems disappearing never to return, three mighty shapes stand
sharply forth, piercing a sky of
royal purple.   Their huge triangular shadows travel slowly
eastward, farther and farther,
as the sun descends,

"Like dials that the wizard, Time,
Had raised to count his ages by."

They are the Pyramids,
whose awful forms have been
enveloped thus in sunset shadows every evening for at least

ANTINOUS.

five thousand years; and when they finally vanish in the
gloom, as most of Egypt's history and glory has been swal-
lowed up in the impenetrable darkness of the past, one realizes that there is no view on earth which can so eloquently
tell him of the grandeur of antiquity and the eternal mystery
of time.

" The Worldly Hope men set their Hearts upon
Turns Ashes—or it prospers; and anon,
Like Snow upon the Desert's dusty Face,
Lighting a little Hour or two—is gone."

Within the citadel of Cairo, only a few steps from the
scene of the massacre of the Mamelukes, is the beautiful
mosque erected by Mehemet Ali, not, as one might suppose,

INTERIOR OF A MOSQUE.

in expiation of his crime, but as the exalted place in which his body should repose. His expectation was fulfilled, and the remains of the talented but cruel Viceroy are sepulchred in a magnificent mausoleum. From the display of oriental alabaster in every portion of this edifice, it has been called the Alabaster Mosque. It has a noble courtyard, with an elaborately decorated fountain, and its proportions are imposing. But its most pleasing architectural feature is its slender minarets, which soar far above the city, resembling silver tapers placed about the Viceroy's tomb.

The tourist soon discovers that the mosque of Mehemet Ali

THE HOUSE OF THE AFRIT.

SOLDIER AND DROMEDARY.

is not the only one in Cairo. On the contrary, mosques are
more numerous in Cairo than churches are in Rome. Connected with most of them are curious superstitions. In one,
for example, two columns are believed to mark the precise spot
where Noah's Ark finally found a resting-place. Nay, not

A STREET SCENE IN CAIRO.

content with this, the legend claims that this is also the
place where Abraham offered up the ram instead of his son
Isaac. These columns, therefore, are supposed to possess
remarkable healing power, and are kept highly polished by
being rubbed with pieces of orange and lemon peel, which

are then applied to diseased portions of the body.   One day
we were much amused to see two men licking these posts
vigorously, in the hope of making their stomachs strong.
This is perhaps the only remedy for dyspepsia not yet adver-
tised in the Occident!

Similar superstitions are associated with one of the oldest
gates of Cairo, the name of which appears in the tales of the
Arabian Nights.   A friend who had lived several years in
Egypt took us one day to see this portal, which is supposed
to be haunted by an *afrit*, or evil spirit.   For some time we
were entertained by watching several old women in succession approach the gate cautiously, spit three times over their
left shoulder, to exorcise the demon, and then peer behind

TOMBS OF THE CALIPHS.

the door with much the same expression that some of their
sex of the Occident assume, when they look timidly under
a bed at night.   Their object was to see if the *afrit* was at
home.   What they might have done if they had discovered

it, would be difficult to conjecture. But the demon was evidently "out" that day,—possibly having been recalled to headquarters. Accordingly the women left what answered for their cards. One, for example, inserted in a crevice of the gate an old tooth, and hobbled off, believing she would thenceforth have no toothache. Another tied to a rusty nail a lock of hair (presumably her own), and smiled to think she would thenceforth be exempt from headache. Thus this demon-haunted portal is kept continually decorated with ghastly teeth and wisps of hair.

It is a curious fact, by the way, that if these people were requested to explain their idea of Satan, they would probably describe him as a blond. A European traveler in Africa relates that the women in one village gathered round him in astonishment, declaring that he was as "white as the Devil." Passing beyond this portal, we found,

NEGLECTED BEAUTY.

outside the city walls, some interesting structures which we recognized as the far-famed tombs of the Caliphs. The name "Caliph," or "Successor," was the title assumed after the Prophet's death by the Mohammedan rulers, some of whom reigned here in magnificence for many years. Even in their ruined condition, we can easily see that these Arabian sepulchres must once have been of exquisite beauty; for the material of many of them is white alabaster, and all their

domes are well-proportioned and ornamented with an arabesque stone tracery so delicate, that one could fancy them to be covered with lace mantles. To see these graceful sepulchres of the Caliphs from a distance in the glow of sunset, is to behold what seems like a mirage of near Saracenic architecture. But approach reveals the fact that they have been allowed to fall into shameful decay, and, incredible as it seems, bats and lizards now infest the beautifully sculptured walls, and families of Egyptian beggars make their homes within the tombs of Mo-

GRACEFUL SEPULCHRES AND HIDEOUS GRAVES.

hammed's successors. On the cracked side of one of them a Persian poet once wrote these words: "Each crevice of this ancient tomb resembles a half-opened mouth, which laughs at the inevitable fate of those who dwell in palaces!"

Around them, and in striking contrast to their former splendor, are hundreds of small gravestones, which mark one of the dreariest places in the world,—a modern Egyptian cemetery. The soil is mere yellow, burning sand, without a flower, tree, or shrub to mitigate its desolation. Moreover, the tombs themselves are hideously plain, consisting of bricks loosely cemented together and surmounted by two sharp-pointed stones. What an added horror must death possess for people who look forward to a burial-place like this!

Beyond these desolate sepulchres, a long avenue of over-arching palm-trees leads us to the site of Heliopolis, that ancient City of the Sun, whose Hebrew name, On, is frequently mentioned in the Old Testament. The Temple of the Sun at Heliopolis was one of the most remarkable that Egypt ever possessed, and its priests were famed throughout the world for their learning. Magnificent presents were given to this sanctuary by Egyptian kings, and its staff of officials, priests, guardians, and servants is said to have numbered nearly thirteen thousand. Joseph married the daughter of a priest of Heliopolis, and here Moses, Pythagoras, Euclid, and Plato received instruction. Yet, on the plain once occupied by this great city, the only relic of it that remains is one majestic obelisk, —the second oldest monument of its kind in existence. Its companion shaft (for obelisks were always placed in pairs) was overthrown eight hundred years ago, and now its

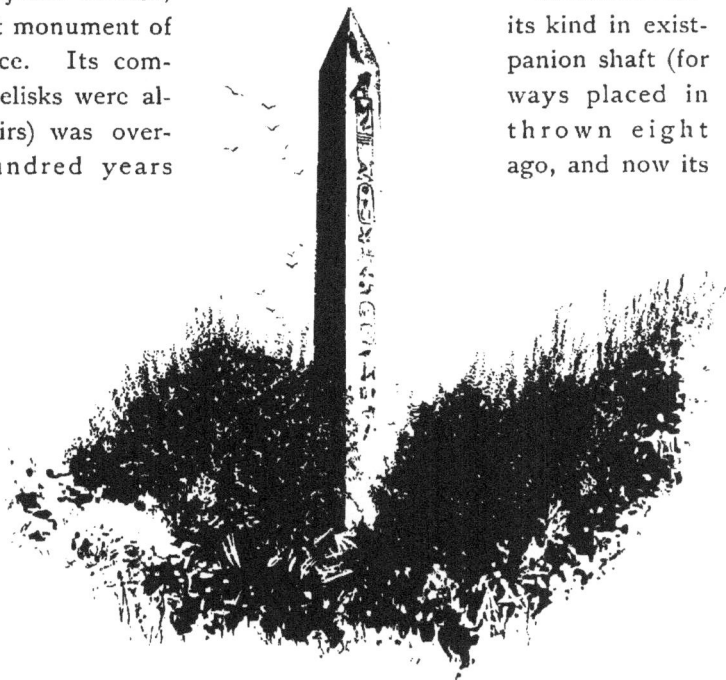

fragments are probably either buried in the vicinity beneath a mass of Nile deposit, or else form part of the foundation of some stately edifice in Cairo. The original beauty of this

AVENUE NEAR CAIRO.

granite monolith must have been striking, for down each of its four sides is a hieroglyphic hymn to the gods, the letters of which were formerly filled with gold, to liken it to the lustre of the sun, since obelisks were used as symbols of the

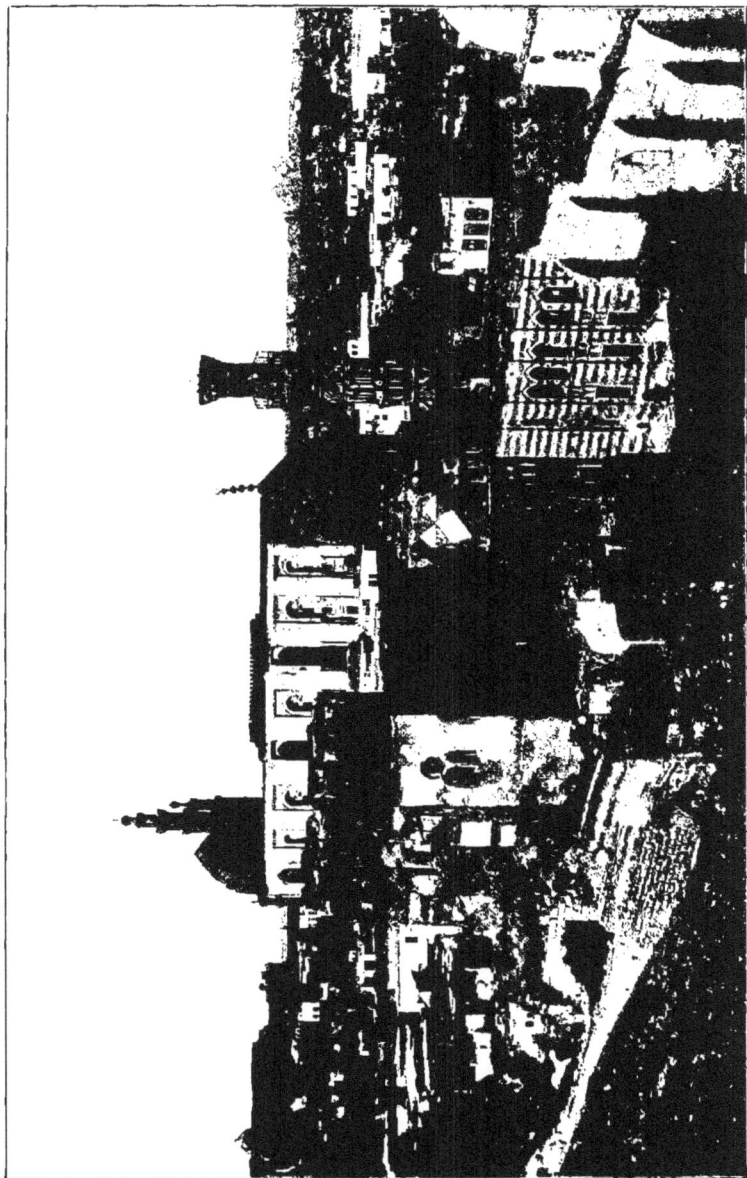

VIEW OF CAIRO.

sun's bright rays. This City of the Sun was doubtless spe-
cially adorned with these tapering shafts, but all the others
have disap-
peared. There
is something
indescribably
mournful in
this, the last
memorial of
Heliopolis, ga-
zing, as it were,
sadly down
from its impo-
sing height up-
on the solitary

THE VIRGIN'S TREE.

plain, so eloquent in its pathetic silence. Moses, no doubt,
looked upon this obelisk; Herodotus and Plato may have
rested in its shadow. Yet upon its sculptured surface, morning and evening, still fall the solar salutations, just as they
did when Rome, Athens, and Jerusalem were the dwelling-
places of barbarians.

PLOWING NEAR HELIOPOLIS.

On the way back from Heliopolis to Cairo, one halts before a famous sycamore, known as the Virgin's Tree, since within its hollow trunk Mary and the Child Jesus are said to have taken refuge during the flight into Egypt. Tradition adds that they would surely have been captured by Herod's agents, had not a spider, after they had entered, covered the opening with its web, thus screening them from discovery. At the inauguration of the Suez Canal, in 1869, the courteous Khedive, Ismail Pasha, presented, of course in jest, this sacred tree to the Empress Eugénie to take back with her to France as a holy relic. It is said that the witty Empress thanked him gravely, but begged him to give her, instead, as a more portable and no less authentic souvenir, the skeleton of the spider that wove the web.

EGYPTIAN RUNNERS.

In the vicinity of Cairo are several delightful drives, through avenues completely sheltered from the sun by stately sycamores and acacias. These are the fashionable promenades of the Egyptian capital, and one of them, called the Shoobra Avenue, is five miles long. Here, every afternoon during the tourist season, one sees in landaus and victorias numberless representatives of different parts of Europe and America, among whom freely mingle wealthy Turks, Arabs, and Egyptians, while not infrequently one catches a glimpse of the Khedive himself or members of his family. It is a curiously cosmopolitan sight, for in the throng of European carriages the fleet little donkeys of Egypt amble along, and gaily caparisoned camels sometimes thrust their heads disdainfully upon the scene and leer at the crowd.

Here, also, one occasionally perceives a characteristic phase of Cairene life in the Nubian Saïs, who runs

AN EGYPTIAN WOMAN.

before the horse or carriage of some rich pasha, and shouts for the way to be cleared. These runners, who are usually as black as ebony, carry wands in their hands, and wear colored turbans, gold-embroidered vests and jackets, and short white skirts, beneath which flash their naked limbs and feet. At frequent intervals we see an officer in handsome uniform, with silver-mounted weapons. These guardians of the peace

SHOOBRA PALACE.

will sometimes condescend to interfere and clear the crowd in case of an entanglement; but usually they content themselves with glaring fiercely at the Europeans, whom they seem to hate, or with posing as royal dignitaries intended for ornament, not for use. But great is the transformation which takes place in them, whenever the Khedive himself rides by. In an instant the scowling and disdainful officer becomes as fawning and obsequious as the veriest slave, and bends his head until the royal equipage is out of sight. He is a perfect illustration of the treacherous servant,— indifferent or tyrannical to those unfortunate enough to be beneath him, — cringing and false to his superiors.

MUSEUM AT CAIRO.

At the end of the Shoobra Avenue is a charming palace of the same name, which is built around an artificial lake, with a marble fountain, resembling an island, in the centre.

What an air of Oriental luxury we seem to breathe, as we stroll along these graceful porticoes! The pavement is of marble mosaic, the ceiling glows with brilliant frescoes, and between them rise, like the trunks of graceful palms, a multitude of slender Moorish columns, reminding one a little of the halls of the Alhambra. The Shoobra Palace was the favorite residence of Mehemet Ali, and even when his hair

MUMMY OF RAMESES II.

and beard were white as snow, the fierce old warrior used to amuse himself here in the oddest fashion. Sitting cross-legged on a comfortable divan, he would watch for hours the adventures of the ladies of his harem, who were, at his command, rowed out upon the lake in gaily colored boats by hideous black eunuchs. Suddenly, at a secret signal given by himself, the boats would be upset and the fair occupants thrown into the water, to be dragged out amid the most ludicrous screams and struggles. At this sight, the old Viceroy would, it is said, put down his coffee-cup or pipe, loll back on his luxurious cushions, and laugh until the tears rolled down his wrinkled cheeks. Strange, is it not, that this grim veteran, stained with the blood of num-

TOMB OF MARIETTE.

berless murdered Mamelukes, could have found pleasure in such childish sport?

At a little distance from the city, on the new driveway to the Pyramids, stands the unrivaled museum of Egyptian antiquities, which a few years ago was transferred hither from the Cairene quarter known as Boulak. It is surrounded by a beautiful garden, within which is the tomb of Mariette, that self-denying and enthusiastic archæologist who gave his life and fortune to Egyptian exploration, and whose untimely death, in 1881, was an irreparable loss to science. While it is literally true that he gave his life to Egypt, in return old

Egypt gave herself to him. For how magnificent was the
success that rewarded his untiring devotion! To have, himself, discovered and rescued from their desert shroud thousands of statues, temples, tombs, and sphinxes,—thus bringing
the beginnings of the recorded history of man within our easy
comprehension,—no doubt abundantly repaid him for long
years of labor and privation. But he had many personal
experiences which must have wonderfully enriched his life.
Thus, close by Memphis, Mariette discovered the famous'
Serapeum, or Cemetery of the Sacred Bulls, all of which,
after death, had been embalmed, and for a period of two
thousand years had rested here in huge sarcophagi of granite,—hidden away for ages under the desert sands. Each of

ROYAL SARCOPHAGI.

the coffins was a monolith weighing nearly sixty tons, and
in these the embalmed bulls were laid away in separate com-
partments in long subterranean galleries, which fill the visitor
with amazement as he looks upon them.

When Mariette opened this vast cemetery, he found one vault which for some reason had escaped the ruthless hands of those who, at some time, inspired by the hope of finding treasure, had plundered most of Egypt's sepulchres. Accord-

ingly, when the portal yielded to his pressure, he perceived in the mortar the signet-impress of the mason who had closed it long before the time of Moses. There also, on a layer of sand, were the footprints of the work-men, who, nearly four thousand years before, had consigned the sacred mummy to its tomb and closed the door, as they sup-posed forever! What wonder, then, that when the great sa-vant found himself thus face to face with a stupendous past, within an area on which no eye

THE VILLAGE CHIEF.

had looked for nearly twice as long a period as had elapsed since Christ was born, he was completely overcome and burst into tears!

An entire lecture might be devoted to the mere enumer-ation of the interesting relics of the Pharaohs contained in this museum; but some mention, at least, must be made of a celebrated statue which, though estimated to be at least four thousand years old, is even now so startlingly lifelike as to astonish all who look upon its face. Its preservation, too, is marvelous, considering that its material is wood. It represents a type of man still common in Egypt. In fact, when it was found, the Arabs were so struck with its resem-blance to their somewhat corpulent overseer, that they immediately called it the "Village Chief," a title which it still retains. What impressed me most about this figure was the expression of its eyes. They fairly haunted me. It seemed as if a living being must dwell within that wooden form, to stare upon me so intently. This effect is due to the peculiar artifice employed in its construction. Thin folds of bronze were used for eyelids, beneath which were inserted, for the eyeballs, pieces of white quartz; the iris was then made of a darker colored stone, while in the centre was driven, for the pupil, a silver nail.

A few miles to the south of Cairo is the site of Memphis, probably the oldest city in Egypt, and the capital of Menes, first of Egypt's kings. We may gain some idea of its antiquity, when we reflect that it was founded, according to Lepsius, four thousand — according to Mariette, five thousand — years before Christ. It is

PALMS NEAR MEMPHIS.

said to have been so large that a half-day's journey was necessary to cross it from north to south; but little of it now remains above ground. A stately palm-grove covers this cradle of the Egyptian dynasties, and silence and soli-

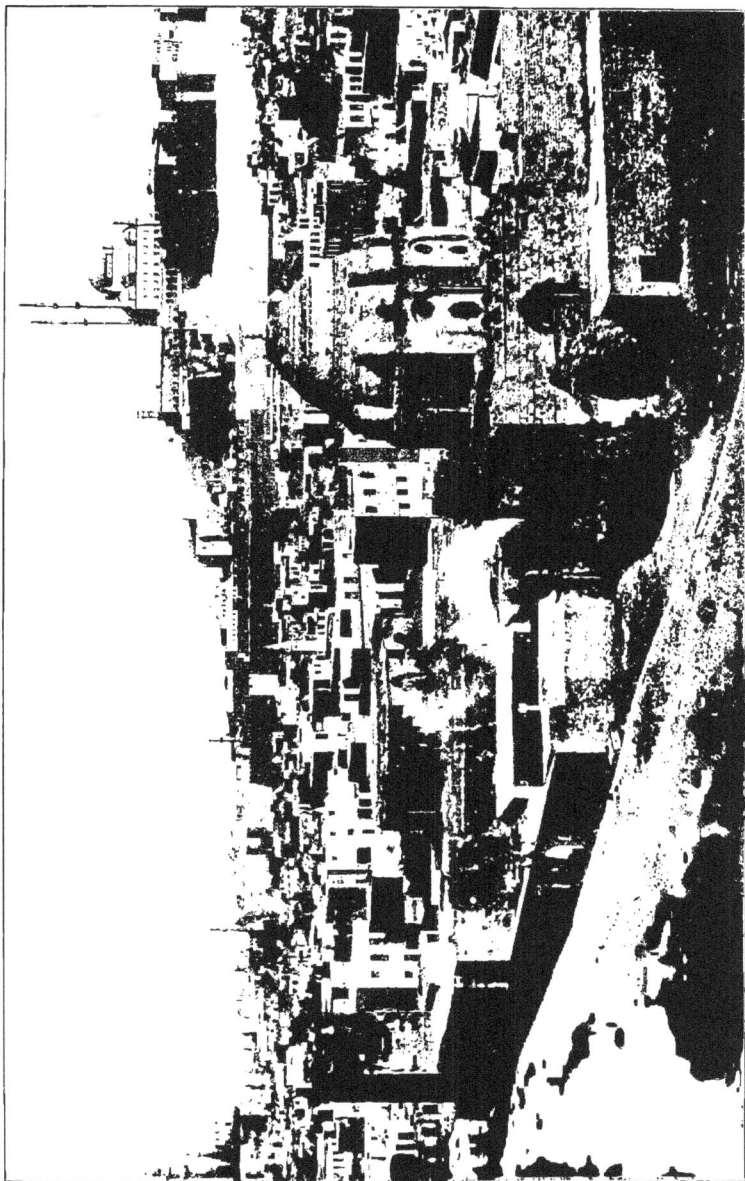

OLD CAIRO AND THE CITADEL.

tude reign here supreme. It is true, Mariette's heroic labors in this region brought to light more than two thousand buried sphinxes, and five thousand statues and tablet-inscriptions. But most of these have been taken away to European museums, and almost the only thing remaining here to-day is a colossal statue of Rameses II, too vast to be removed. This now lies prostrate on its finely sculptured face, commingling slowly with historic dust.

Never shall I forget an afternoon which I spent on the site

THE SITE OF MEMPHIS.

of Memphis, seated within its stately palm-grove, on the border of the adjoining desert. Here, for the first time, I seemed to realize that I was in the land of the Pharaohs. The subtile influence of Egyptian antiquity stole insensibly upon me, until I seemed to have been carried back to the days of Abraham; and the long trains of loaded camels, the turbaned Arabs, the half-veiled women, the tufted palm-trees, and the silent desert, ceased finally to fill me with astonishment, and seemed fitting accessories to the scene before me.

While seated here that day, I watched for some time an Arab riding across the shining expanse of the desert, the soft, cushioned feet of his camel sinking into the sand with a

ARAB AT PRAYER.

solemn, noiseless tread. It was the hour of prayer. Far off upon the minarets of Cairo the muezzins were proclaiming the sacred formula of Islam. Dismounting, the rider bound the foreleg of his camel, planted his lance beside him in the sand, and then, turning his face toward sacred Mecca, performed his devotions. As I watched him, I could but feel that we were in the grandest of all earthly temples, beside which Santa Sophia and St. Peter's dwindled to pygmies; for its golden pavement was the measureless sweep of the Sahara,—its dome, the canopy of heaven.

To a person floating in a balloon over Egypt, the country would

STATUE OF RAMESES II.

THE MAJESTIC NILE.

present the ap-
pearance of a
long strip of
green carpet
spread out upon
a sandy floor.
For, as it seldom
rains here, the
entire country
would be a des-
ert, were it not
for the annual
inundation of
the Nile, which
rescues from the
sand on either side of the river a narrow fringe of territory;
and both these river-banks, although hemmed in by scorching
deserts, glow nevertheless with beauty and fertility because of
the alluvial deposit of this fruitful overflow.

The Nile is, in fact, the artery of Egypt, upon whose
regular pulsa-
tions the exist-
ence of the land
depends.   The
loam in the
Egyptian Del-
ta is that riv-
er's sediment,

Between the fertile valley, thus created and renewed, and the adjoining desert a ceaseless warfare is waged,—the old, eternal struggle between Life and Death. To the Egyptians this river represented the creative principle, just as the desert symbolized destruction. In the mythology of Egypt there is a pretty fable, to the effect that the crystal springs of the Nile bubble up in the gardens of Paradise and serve for the ablutions of angels. Thence, wandering through

THE INUNDATION.

lovely meadows, the infant stream finally expands into this lordly and majestic river, which offers life and plenty to the world.

Within the arches of the Vatican there now reclines in Oriental calm an ancient statue of old Father Nile, leaning upon a miniature sphinx; while on its shoulders and around its limbs play sixteen pygmies, representing the sixteen cubits of the annual rise of the river. Surely it is not strange that the old Egyptians deified the Nile, to whose life-bringing flood they owed not only their sustenance, but the very soil on which they lived. Of all the rivers in the world this is the most extraordinary. Some of its characteristics seem almost supernatural. For the last fifteen hundred miles of its course,— that is to say, for nearly one half of its entire length,— it receives no tributary whatever, but flows on calmly beneath a burning sun,

A NATIVE RAFT.

and with a stony wilderness on either side. Yet, notwithstanding all its loss, not only by evaporation in that torrid atmosphere, but by the canals which lure its fruitful flood to the right and left, by the absorption of its sandy banks, and

FATHER NILE.

finally by the draughts made upon it by the countless mouths of men and beasts from Nubia to the sea, it seems at last to pour into the Mediterranean a broader and more copious stream than it displayed a thousand miles away! Nor is this all. Ordinarily an inundation causes calamity and inspires terror; but the overflow of the great river of Egypt is hailed with thanks-

giving. Songs of rejoicing are heard along its rapidly disappearing banks, and its advancing waves are hailed as harbingers
of peace and plenty. To the wretched fellaheen of Egypt, a
few feet more or less of water in the rise of the Nile makes
all the difference between abject poverty and comparative
plenty; since, whenever the water-supply is scanty, the desert remorselessly advances, to swallow up the fields, where in
good years luxuriant crops are wont to gladden the eye.

NILE BRIDGE AT CAIRO.

The Egyptian peasant would be not a little surprised to
learn that we of the Occident depend for our vegetation upon
water falling from the clouds. To him, who rarely sees a
drop of rain, this would seem a very precarious mode of
agriculture. The rise of water in the Upper Nile com-
mences in the month of February. By March, it is percepti-
ble at Khartoum, at Dongola in April, and on the Delta in
the month of May. It usually reaches its full height early in
September, remains thus for a fortnight, and then gradually

TRAVELING ON THE NILE.

subsides. At its climax,—when the river has attained a height of about twenty-four feet above low water-level,—the valley looks like an archipelago studded with green islands, each of which is crowned with palm-trees and a little village. Then, when the waters subside, the country clothes itself at once in vegetation, and Mother Earth appears as young and beautiful as when the Pyramids first gazed upon the wondrous scene.

No visit to Egypt is now complete which does not include a journey on the Nile, at least as far as the site of ancient "hundred-gated" Thebes, six hundred miles inland from the Mediterranean. At present the tourist can choose between two

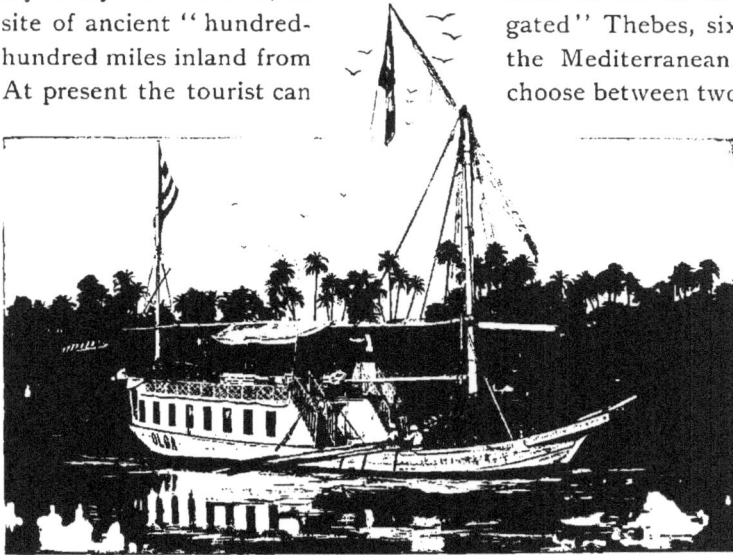

A DAHABIYEH.

modes of travel on this river. One is by an excursion steamer, which involves a tour of several weeks with a promiscuous company; the other is by a "dahabiyeh," or private boat, where one selects his own companions and is entirely independent,—a dragoman furnishing food, servants, and crew for the entire journey. The great majority of Egyptian tourists take the steamer, which is certainly swift, well-managed, comfortable, and less expensive than a private boat. On the other

A FLOATING HOME.

hand, if time and money are of no particular consideration, and if one wishes to arrange his visits to the different ruins of the Upper Nile with greater freedom and with more seclusion than can be obtained if he is traveling by the schedule time of a crowded tourist-steamer, he would do well to take a dahabiyeh. Certainly those who love reading and tranquillity, and are interested in Egyptian history and antiquities, need not fear the longer duration of the journey occasioned by the use of a private boat. A fair

PROMENADE OF THE HAREM.

allowance being made for individual tastes and temperaments, I believe it to be a fact that upon no equal period of the traveler's life will he look back with more un-alloyed enjoyment than upon the weeks or months passed in profound tran-quillity and delicious revery, gliding along the golden rim of the Sahara, which seems a well-nigh

CLEOPATRA.

endless avenue leading him back through a mirage of myths and legends into the very dawn of history. What memories

ANTONY AND CLEOPATRA.

recur to him, as his boat cleaves the current of this ruin-bordered stream! Its revelries, for example,—upon how many did

ON THE NILE.

Egypt's cloudless sun and lustrous moon look down, when the most fascinating woman of antiquity,— the irresistible siren of the Nile,— was wont to sail upon the surface of this same majestic stream, accompanied by Antony, in a gilded barge whose perfumed sails swelled languidly with the breezes of the Orient.

Little did they then anticipate the tragic death-scene that awaited them when they should have drained to the dregs their golden goblet of life and love!

These and a hundred other incidents connected with Egyptian history are, on a

THE SCULPTURED LOTUS.

voyage like this, continually suggested to us by memory, reading, and conversation; and are all emphasized in a most

charming and impressive way, whenever we land to inspect
at various points the awe-inspiring relics of antiquity. ''He
who has once tasted the water of the Nile,'' says an Arab
proverb, ''longs for it inexpressibly forevermore.''

It would exceed the scope of this volume to enumerate
all the ruined temples which the tourist passes in sailing up
the Nile. It is interesting, however, to observe that almost
all the columns of these ancient shrines terminate in the
sculptured bell of the lotus flower,—an ornament that gives
lightness to these ponderous masses, and seems to be the

LUXOR.

appropriate coronation of the columnar stem. Many of these
chiseled lotus blossoms are just as perfect now as when they
left the sculptor's hand; and even when mutilated by some
vandal, their broken edges look like the crumpled petals of a
flower, still blooming on from century to century. It is fitting that we should see Egypt's favorite blossom represented
in her temples, for the poets of antiquity sang of the far-
famed lotus that grew on the banks of the Nile, and claimed
that if the traveler ate of it he at once forgot home and kin-
dred, and lingered ever on this distant shore.

Next to the region of the Pyramids and Sphinx, the most
attractive part of Egypt is the site of Thebes, the principal

destination of all travelers who ascend the Nile. More than four thousand years ago there lay here, as there lies to-day, a mighty plain, cut by the Nile into two equal parts. Upon this plain was an Egyptian city that must have been to the

TEMPLE OF RAMESES.

ancient world what Rome was in the days of Hadrian. It so abounded in stupendous palaces and temples, that even their ruins are to-day the marvel of the world, and draw to them admiring travelers from every land. One of the most extraordinary of these structures is the temple built by Rameses II, which was a ruin long before most of the other ancient edifices of the world were reared. It was demolished by the Persian conqueror, Cambyses, six centuries before Christ, and only a few of its enormous columns are now standing, though everywhere we see the pedestals of many more. Some of its walls were supported by massive statues thirty feet in height, which are now headless and otherwise disfigured; and yet their folded arms still give to them an air of grandeur and mystery, as if they were guarding faithfully in their locked breasts the secrets of unnumbered ages.

Beside these standing giants, however, lies one whose mere fragments dwarf them all. It is the overthrown statue

RAISING WATER FROM THE NILE.

of King Rameses, the largest sculptured figure in the world. This monster, once a solid block of beautifully polished granite, measures twenty-six feet across the shoulders, and its weight, when entire, must have been nearly nine hundred tons. Yet it was transported hither over a distance of one hundred and fifty miles. It is alike difficult to understand how such a colossus could have been quarried, brought hither, or broken, as we now find it. An earthquake could hardly have shattered it so completely. Such devastation could only have been effected by the vandalism of man. Upon its surface were inscribed the words —"I am the king of kings. If any one wishes to know how great I am, let him try to surpass one of my works." But now, like Lucifer hurled from Heaven, the mighty Rameses lies overthrown, and several millstones have been cut from his head, without perceptibly diminishing the size.

A visit to another portion of the Theban city revealed to us the two colossal figures which photographic art has made familiar to the world. They

THE OVERTHROWN STATUE.

are both sadly mutilated, but seated as they are, and have been for so many ages, in solitude and silence on this historic plain, they look like the abandoned deities of the place, whom grief has turned to stone. They do not, however,

THE VOCAL MEMNON.

really represent deities; they are the statues of King Amunoph III, and were originally placed here before the entrance of his temple. Each of these figures is a monolith, fifty-two feet in height without the pedestal, and weighs about eight hundred tons! It is true, they do not look like monoliths now, for one can see a multitude of different blocks composing their arms and shoulders. But both were solid masses of stone till they were riven by an earthquake shock twenty-seven years before Christ; and two hundred years later, the Roman Emperor Septimius Severus clumsily restored them. This fact of their restoration explains the mystery of the voice which the more northern of these *colossi*, called by the Greeks the "Vocal Memnon," was believed to possess, since every morning, at sunrise, there would issue from it a peculiar sound, which

THE COLOSSI OF THEBES.

A DERVISH DRUM.

was interpreted as being a salutation to the god of day. In the early years of the Christian era this was deemed so wonderful that Greek and Roman travelers made a journey up the Nile to look upon this statue and to hear its "voice," with almost as much interest as they felt in visiting the Pyramids and the Sphinx.

For many years the usual explanation of this phenomenon was that of fraud. It was supposed that a priest concealed himself in the statue, and at sunrise, by striking the stone with a metallic hammer, produced the sound which awed into amazement the worshipers of old. But, on the other hand it seems incredible that for two hundred years priests could climb into this statue every night and climb down again every day, and never be discovered. Obviously, this colossus could not, like a chess automaton, be rolled away occasionally from the stage, for it stood out boldly on the plain, and could be watched continually by thousands. Nor was its voice immemorial. The statue had stood here for fifteen hundred years before it became vocal. It was only after its injury by the earthquake that its voice began to be heard. It then continued musical for two hundred and twenty years; but as soon as it was repaired by the Roman emperor,—that is, as soon as its crevices were filled with stone and plaster, — it became dumb

AN EGYPTIAN HEAD-DRESS.

again, and has remained so ever since. It would seem con-
clusive, therefore, that the mysterious sound which puzzled
all antiquity, was due to the warmth of the rising sun acting
on the mass of cracked and sundered stone, which had been
thoroughly chilled and moistened with dew during the night,
—a fact not without a parallel in some peculiar rock forma-
tions of the world.

On the opposite
bank of the Nile
to that on which
the Vocal Memnon
and his comrade
sit alone, stands
the most wonder-
ful of all the edi-
fices of old Thebes,
the temple of Kar-
nak. It forms, in
fact (with the ex-
ception of the Pyr-
amids), the largest
and most imposing
ruin, not only in

APPROACH TO KARNAK.

Egypt, but in the world. The approach to this was formerly
by an avenue nearly two miles long, lined with at least two
thousand colossal sphinxes, crouching side by side, fragments
of which are still discernible. Between them, so long ago as
the time of Joseph, passed with reverent tread unnumbered
worshipers, who must have been overwhelmed with awe by

GATEWAY OF KARNAK.

the grandeur of this unrivaled vestibule.   To-day Arab beggars sun themselves here in the sand.   Some one has said
that it is fortunate for these sphinxes that they are beheaded,
since they are spared the sight of the temple's degradation.
Beyond them one perceives, from a great distance, a solitary
portal.   Beneath it giants might have passed, for it is seventy

"WILD CONFUSION."

feet in height.   Compared to it, a man appears to be a pygmy.
Time seems to have favored certain portions of this ruined
shrine, and this is one of them; for, preserved in the wonderfully clear atmosphere of Egypt and the unvarying sunshine
of the Nile, it stands at present in its stately beauty almost
as perfect as when its lofty arch resounded to the murmur of
adoring thousands.

IN KARNAK.

Passing through this gigantic outer gate, we paused with bated breath before a glimpse of Karnak itself. Who can ever forget his first view of this temple, whose walls are eighty feet in height, some of whose towers reach an altitude of one hundred and forty feet, and whose vast area is a mile and a half in circumference? Before us was a wild confusion of mammoth columns, cyclopean walls, and towering obelisks. It seemed to be a ruined city, rather than a temple, reduced to chaos by an earthquake. One feels that he is standing here upon a battlefield, where Time has struggled with the products of human genius. With whom the victory has rested, the mutilated remains upon the plain significantly prove.

Making our way through this bewildering

AN AISLE IN KARNAK.

labyrinth, we approached one of the smaller avenues of Karnak. How well preserved the columns are! And yet in point of age they are as far removed in one direction from the birth of Christ, as we are in the other. Despite their history of four thousand years, these columns wear no ivied wreaths of age, and had not the ruthless hands of iconoclasts been raised against them, they would doubtless have remained intact to the present day. One realizes here that the Egyptians built their

A BIT OF KARNAK.

temples, not for centuries, but for ages. In fact, one of the inscriptions on these walls states that the king Rameses confidently counts upon the gods for help, because he has reared to them "eternal mountains."

The columns, first met with as one approaches Karnak, enormous though they are, sink to comparative insignificance, when we enter the main avenue of the temple. No illustrations or statistics can give an adequate idea of the majesty of such architecture as this. Yet in one hall alone are no less than a hundred and thirty-four columns, some of which are thirty-six feet in circumference and sixty-six feet high, while many of the solid blocks which they support are forty feet in length. The lotus flowers which crown them are so vast that twelve men can, with outstretched arms, and hands pressed finger-tip to finger-tip, barely enclose one of their curving lips. What wonder that the Arabs declared that the ancient Egyptians were giants, who had the power

ETERNAL MOUNTAINS.

of moving at will cyclopean masses of stone, as by the mere stroke of the enchanter's wand?

On entering another shadowy aisle of Karnak, we found that conquerors had sought to overthrow some of these mighty pillars. In several instances the miscreant vandals were successful; but one huge shaft refused to fall, and, although started from its foundation, it leans against its neighbor (one fancies wearily and painfully), as though it were a giant's dislocated limb. However, we can safely walk beneath this leaning column, for it has been thus deflected since before the time of Christ.

Soulless indeed must be the traveler who can walk among the ruins of Karnak without emotions too profound for words.

In the whole world there is no temple that can be even remotely compared to it. It must have been even more impressive, when its vast aisles were covered with a roof, which, if we may judge from other Egyptian ceilings that remain, was probably painted a deep blue, to represent the cloudless sky of Egypt, and glittered with a thousand golden stars. Even now the daylight, streaming down through this forest of columns, reveals to us pictorial

A CORRIDOR.

carvings twenty feet in height, with a multitude of sacred characters, cut several inches deep into the solid stone, each

THE LEANING COLUMN.

letter polished to its entire depth and colored like mosaic. These are not fanciful and meaningless decorations, but hymns of praise to kings and gods, as perfectly comprehended in those times as Latin sentences are to-day.

Until 1799, Egyptian hieroglyphics were a mystery, but at the close of the eighteenth century these sacred writings of past ages were made plain by the discovery of a tablet of black basalt (called the " Rosetta Stone " after the town near which it was found), which was dug out of the soil of the Delta. Upon this stone, which is about four feet in height, was inscribed in three languages a decree issued by the Egyptian priesthood at Memphis, about two hundred years before

THE ROSETTA STONE.

Christ. One of these languages was Greek, the other two were, respectively, the priestly and the popular writing of the Egyptians. By a comparison of the known Greek with the unknown Egyptian characters, a key was found by which to decipher the priestly symbols of the Pharaohs. To Champollion, the distinguished French linguist, is due unstinted praise for this great work, without which the reading of the monuments of ancient Egypt and even the comprehension of Egyptian history would have been impossible. As is well known, the Rosetta Stone now forms one of the most valued treasures of the British Museum.

Time, the destroyer, can apparently lay no hand on sculptures such as these. They still remain, and will no doubt remain for centuries to come, illumined tablets of history, as perfect as when they were beheld through clouds of incense by the assembled worshipers of old.

In strolling through the immense area of Karnak's ruins, we frequently discovered stately obelisks which were hewn from the primitive volcanic granite nearly forty centuries ago. One of these, which, as the inscription tells us, was once surmounted by a little pyramid of gold, is ninety-two

OBELISKS AT KARNAK.

feet high and eight feet square. Some of these monoliths are prostrate, while others are erect; but whether prone or perpendicular, amid these wonderful surroundings, and with the secrets of past ages graven on their sides, they are unusually impressive memorials of the heroes of the past, and

" Like a right-arm lifted towards the sky,
    Each obelisk makes oath their memory shall not die."

Though Karnak is the most stupendous ruin of Upper Egypt, by far the loveliest is the island of Philæ, encircled by the glittering Nile. It is an uninhabited island now, only twelve hundred feet in length and five hundred in breadth,

PHILÆ.

but the memories it awakens are like precious jewels in a tiny casket,—"infinite riches in a little room." This "Pearl of the Nile," as it is called, now fringed with palms and crowned with ruined temples, was formerly sacred to the goddess Isis, the mightiest of the Egyptian Trinity; and here her worship was continued secretly, long after the decrees of Christian emperors had elsewhere abolished the old faith of Egypt.

For centuries before that time, however, the templed isle of Isis was the resort of countless travelers and pilgrims, by whom it was as much revered as is the Holy Sepulchre at Jerusalem by the majority of Christians to-day; for this was supposed to be the burial-place of Osiris, the husband of Isis; and the most sacred oath of the Egyptians was the phrase, "By him who sleeps in Philæ."

At one extremity of this island is an exquisite little structure known as "Pharaoh's Bed." It is difficult to imagine anything architecturally more beautiful than this graceful pavilion, outlined against the glorious blue sky of Upper Egypt. It is not, however, very ancient, as things go in Egypt, having been built by the Roman emperor Tiberius, about the time of Christ. How Egypt dwarfs all lands and ruins which we have previously called ancient! In Britain we survey with wonder its old cathedrals, built six

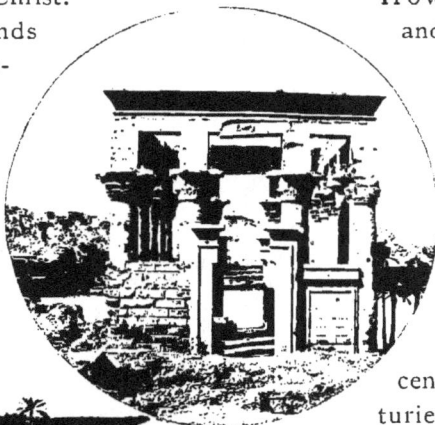

PHARAOH'S BED.

centuries ago; in Italy we are thrilled by scenes reminding us of Roman life and customs eighteen hundred years since; in Athens we go back still farther.

But here upon the changeless Nile, when once accustomed to its antiquity, we find ourselves exclaiming lightly: "Oh, this is merely Greek," or "That is as modern as the Cæsars."

If the island of Philæ is beautiful by day, by night it has a fascination almost beyond the power of language to describe. For when the moon threads these deserted avenues with silver sandals; holding her pale light, here and there, for us to note these sculptured chronicles of kings,

PHILÆ BY MOONLIGHT.

beautiful Philæ rises once more in its splendor, its sculptures speaking to us of the vanished Isis and Osiris, in that mysterious language of dead ages whose books were the temples of the gods, the leaves of which were blocks of stone.

Most tourists on the Nile are content to go no farther than the first cataract and Philæ; but those who journey still farther southward into Nubia are abundantly repaid by one

PHILÆ. — PEARL OF THE NILE.

of the most awe-inspiring of Egyptian ruins,—the temple of
Abou-Simbel. This edifice, which is cut for a distance of
three hundred feet into the rocky hillside by the river, is now
half-buried in drifts of shining sand. Beside it are four
statues of Rameses II, of such prodigious size, that the huge
door, although enormous in itself, seems small beside them.
This portal conducts the traveler into a subterranean hall,
where are still other monster statues, waiting with folded

ABOU-SIMBEL.

arms through
the slow-moving
centuries, like
captive giants
whom only a ter-
rific earthquake
shock can liber-
ate. Torchlight
reveals an altar
where sacrifices
were offered to
the gods more
than three thou-
sand years ago.

One of the
exterior statues
is mutilated beyond recognition, but all of them represented
the same monarch. The position of the hands on the knees
is characteristic of most royal Egyptian statues, and is sym-
bolic of Rameses resting after his conquest of the then known
world. It is not strange that the Egyptians gave to him the
title, "King of Kings," for he was really the greatest conqueror of antiquity, prior to the era of Greece and Rome.
He was apparently a favorite of fortune, living to the age of
eighty-seven, and ruling Egypt for no less than sixty-seven
years. It was his passion to erect magnificent temples, and

place in front of them some of those obelisks and statues which, after all they have survived, are still the marvel of the world. Nor were these ornamental works the only monuments which Rameses bequeathed to Egypt, for he caused the stony desert to be pierced in various places with artesian wells; he finished a canal connecting the Mediterranean and the Red Sea, more than three thousand years before De Lesseps followed in his footsteps; while, as a warrior, he had conquered Syria and seized upon the fortress of Jerusalem more than a hundred years before the Israelites (led out from Egypt during the reign of his successor) set foot upon the soil of Palestine.

But to appreciate adequately the vastness of these statues at Abou-Simbel, we should examine them singly. Each is no less than sixty-six feet high, and its forefinger is a yard in length. If the figure stood erect, it would

A NUBIAN WOMAN.

reach an altitude of nearly eighty-three feet. A group of travelers standing on its lap looks like a swarm of insects resting on its surface. The lower half of the leg measures twenty feet from knee to heel. The destruction of one of these statues was effected more than two thousand years ago by foreign conquerors; but what a comment upon human nature it is, that such sublime monuments, after enduring for so many ages, should now, without the excuse of foreign conquest, be disgracefully mutilated by modern travelers, who (itching for notoriety) have placed upon these ruins their names, and those of the towns unfortunate enough to be their birthplaces. Some of these carvings, in letters a foot in length, have been actually filled in with paint! A few years ago a traveler took a plas-

A CONTRAST.

ter cast of one of the heads, and left it besmeared with whitewash, which he had not the decency to efface. Alas! almost

PART OF ONE STATUE.

all of Egypt's unique treasures have suffered from the wanton depredations of man. Not long ago a party of tourists visited the grand old obelisk at Heliopolis, which was already ancient when Abraham made his journey into Egypt, and were found knocking pieces out of it with an axe! When one hears of such vandalism, one can agree with Douglas Jerrold, who, while arguing that every kind of business had its pleasant side, remarked: "If I were an undertaker, I know of several persons whom I could work for with considerable satisfaction."

THE STATUES OF RAMESES II.

The most impressive view of Abou-Simbel is that which reveals these seated statues from a distance, in profile. Gigantic as their features are, they nevertheless possess a serene, majestic beauty, which becomes marvelous when we reflect that these colossal figures were hewn directly from the face of the mountain. Surely such forms and features, cut thus from the natural rock, were the work of men whose

genius was akin
to that of Mi-
chael Angelo.
There was to
me something
indescribably
weird and un-
earthly in their
solemn faces
forever gazing
at the river,
with an expres-
sion which has
not changed
while ages have
flowed on be-

BEDOUINS AT THE PYRAMIDS.

neath them, like the stream itself. They look as if they had
the power to rise, if they desired, and tell us of the awful
mysteries on which their lips are sealed.

Notwithstanding the marvelous character of the ruins of
the Upper Nile, nothing in Egypt so appeals to our imagination and enthusiasm as those incomparable memorials of the

APPROACH TO THE PYRAMIDS.

Pharaohs,—the Pyramids and Sphinx. They are easily accessible from Cairo, as a fine carriage-road now leads almost to their base. On my first visit to them, more than a score of years ago, the Arabs who infest their vicinity were by no means as well disciplined as they are to-day. No sooner had we reached the edge of the desert, than we were

SECTION OF A PYRAMID.

assailed by numbers of vociferous Bedouins, who, in their long white gowns, resembled African somnambulists. All clamored fiercely for the privilege of conducting us to the summit of the Great Pyramid; but our guide treated them with indifference, until we were surrounded by perhaps sixty men, who shouted and gesticulated as if they were demented. Then he called upon the chief of these madmen to appoint two for each of us. This was finally done amid the wildest confusion. The rejected men acted like petulant children, lying down in the sand, throwing it into the air, howling, and doing other foolish acts indicative of their chagrin.

At length, the disappointed ones, seeing a new party of travelers approach, started off like a troop of wild beasts to meet them, thus giving us an opportunity to look up quietly at the prodigious structures, which are apparently destined to perish only with the world.

No view does justice to the Pyramids, but the world contains nothing of human workmanship quite so imposing. They stand upon the border of the desert, as other ruins lie beside the sea. Their vast triangular forms, with bases covered by the golden sand, and summits cleaving wedge-

A CORNER OF CHEOPS.

like the serene blue sky, exceed, when seen thus close at hand, the most extravagant expectations. A comprehensive idea can not be obtained from statistics, but one must make use of figures and comparisons to give to those who have not seen them some adequate conception of the immensity of these masses of stone. The original height of the Pyramid of Cheops was four hundred and eighty-two feet. About thirty feet of its apex has disappeared, but even now it is higher than the top of St. Peter's; and if this pyramid were hollow, the vast

basilica at Rome could be placed within it, dome and all, like
an ornament in a glass case! St. Paul's in London could
then in turn be easily placed inside of St. Peter's, for the top
of its dome is one hundred feet lower than the summit of the
Great Pyramid.   Each of its sides measures at the base seven
hundred and sixty-four feet. If its materials were torn down, they would suffice to build around the whole frontier of France a parapet ten feet high and a foot and a half thick. Think of a field of thirteen acres completely covered with eighty-five million cubic feet of solid masonry, piled together with such precision and accuracy

AN EGYPTIAN SHEIK.

that astronomical calculations have been based on its angles
and shadows, since the mighty pile was built exactly facing
the cardinal points of the compass! This solidity of structure
and immensity of mass would seem to assure to the Pyramids
a well-nigh endless existence.   "All things," it is said, "fear
Time, but Time fears the Pyramids."

VILLAGE NEAR THE PYRAMIDS.

Among the various conflicting theories regarding the origin and meaning of the Great Pyramid, one thing may certainly be affirmed : its royal builder did not intend to have

PYRAMID OF CEPHREN.

it used as a gymnasium by tourists, though scores of them ascend it every day. The difficulty in climbing it is owing to the height of the steps to be taken, varying as they do from two to four feet, according to the broken or perfect condition of the stone. In ascending it, I made my two Arab attendants fully earn their money. Giving a hand to

THE BASE OF CHEOPS.

each, and stipulating that we should go slowly, I was pulled quite comfortably to the top of Cheops in about fifteen minutes, and found the summit to be at present a rocky platform about thirty feet square. One should not grumble, however, at the difficulty of making this ascent, for it is owing to their broken surfaces that one is able to climb the Pyramids at all. On near approach they seem like gigantic flights of stairs. But originally each presented a perfectly smooth exterior, the

PYRAMID OF SAKKARAH.

spaces between the steps being filled with stone blocks, fitted with the utmost nicety. The whole pyramid was then covered with cement and beautifully polished. In fact, the second largest pyramid, Cephren, —almost a rival of Cheops,—

has still around its apex a remnant of the polished coating, which makes it very difficult to reach the summit. Centuries ago, however, most of these covering blocks were carried off to build the mosques and palaces of Cairo.

What was the purpose in erecting these structures? Are they simply monuments of national or royal vanity? Are they memorials of Egyptian victories or conquests? Not at all. Incredible as it may seem, they are merely the colossal sepulchres of kings—the most enormous ever reared by man. It was customary to build pyramids here as late as the time of Abraham, twenty-three hundred years before Christ; but, at a subsequent period, when the capital of the Pharaohs had been transferred from Memphis up the Nile to Thebes, rock-hewn sepulchres seem to have been preferred. Cheops is not the oldest of Egyptian pyramids. That of Sakkarah, a few miles away, probably antedates it by five hundred years. The whole region for more than forty miles is honeycombed with sepulchres, and it was all the cemetery of Memphis,—that splendid capital whose tombs have long outlived its palaces and temples.

The graves in this vast necropolis, including the pyramids, are, like the tombs at Thebes, all found on the west bank of the Nile,—the side associated with those emblems of mortality, the desert and the setting sun. It is a solemn fact, therefore, that what remains to us of ancient Egypt has to do with death, not life, and was constructed with reference not to time but to eternity. The palaces and capitals of Egypt's kings have almost vanished from the earth; even their sites are often matters of conjecture; but the stupendous temples of the gods, the rock-hewn tombs, and the long line of giant sepulchres built in the form of pyramids, still survive, to emphasize the triumph of the eternal over the temporal.

EGYPTIAN FUNERAL CEREMONIES.

The Greeks rightly said of the Egyptians, that they looked upon their earthly dwelling as a kind of inn, but upon the grave as their eternal home. In fact, they did make far more elaborate preparations for death than for life. Each

PYRAMID OF CHEOPS.

of the Pharaohs, as soon as he ascended the throne, began to build his mausoleum (usually in pyramidal form), and from his neighboring palace in Memphis proudly watched its progress and embellishment. The pyramid of Cheops is not, therefore, as some have ingeniously argued, entirely different from the rest,—a structure built by inspiration of God, and intended to preserve for the race a perfect standard of measurement, or to prophesy by a certain number of inches the year of the world's destruction. There is no reason to doubt that it is the mausoleum of one of a long line of monarchs, all of whom erected similar, though smaller, tombs. It seems, indeed, too vast to be a casket for one human body; yet that same body, when alive, had power to order such a structure to be built, and doubtless thought it none too massive and imposing for his sepulchre.

The summit of Cheops affords a view unequaled in the world. Hundreds of miles to the westward stretches the

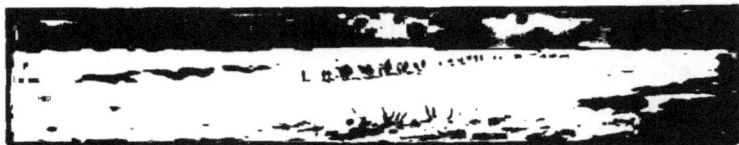

THE SAHARA.

vast Sahara, scattering its first golden sands at the very base of the pyramids. It is an awful sight from its dreary immensity. With its rolling waves of sand it seems a petrified ocean suddenly transformed from a state of activity into one of eternal rest. Far away, upon its yellow surface, the sunlit tents of a Bedouin encampment glisten like whitecaps on a rolling sea. In truth, this vast Sahara is an ocean—of sand. It has the same succession of limitless horizons and the same dreary monotony. Dromedaries glide over its sand waves,—true "ships of the desert," as they are called.

SHIPS OF THE DESERT.

Along its sunlit surface caravans come and go like fleets of commerce. Finally, like the ocean, it is often lashed by storms which sweep it with resistless force, raising its tawny waves to blind, overwhelm, and suffocate the wretched traveler who may encounter them, until he falls, coffined only in the shroud of sand woven around him by the pitiless storm-king.

On my last visit to Egypt, this solemn area of antiquity was spoiled for me in the daytime by the great crowd of travelers assembled in and about the hotel recently built almost within the shadow of the Pyramids. Serious contemplation and a true appreciation of these monuments are quite impossible in a place where one or two hundred polyglot guests are eating lunch, enlivened by the strains of Strauss' waltzes. It is the most glaring illustration of bad taste and mercenary greed that I have ever seen; and if the rest of Egypt were disfigured by such scandalous anachronisms, I should not wish ever again to set foot on its soil. Accordingly, my only satisfactory visit to the Pyramids and Sphinx, under the present condition of affairs in Egypt, was made at midnight and by moonlight. Then, with but one companion,

TEMPLE OF THE SPHINX.

and freed alike from crowds of noisy tourists and importunate Bedouins, and lighted only by the moon and stars, I spent four memorable hours beside these architectural mementoes of a vanished race, until the radiance of the dawn stole up the eastern sky and flushed the face of the expectant Sphinx.

When standing on the summit of the Great Pyramid, if we look below us, we see what seems to be an immense, yawning grave. It is the temple of the Sphinx, partly exhumed by Mariette from the desert sands. Within it were discovered nine statues of King Cephren, the builder of the second pyramid. From this circumstance it is probable that he was its founder, and from its situation in the Necropolis of Memphis we may conclude that this shrine was used for funeral ceremonies. But now it is itself half-sepulchred in

THE SPHINX.

the mighty desert. Its altars are abandoned; the feet of thousands no longer tread its pavement; and if its epitaph could be traced above it in the shifting sand, it might appropriately read: "All who tread the globe are but a handful to the tribes that slumber in its bosom." *

What thrills one as he stands upon the soil of Egypt—rich beyond computation with the spoils of time,—is the mysterious conception that it gives of all the unknown Past which must have here preceded Memphis and the Pyramids. The progress of the race in different lands from barbarism to a state of advanced civilization, has always been a slow and painful one. Unless the Egyptians, therefore, were a notable exception to this rule, they must have existed here for tens of centuries before attaining the degree of culture which was evidently theirs more than six thousand years ago. From manuscripts discovered in their tombs and temples, we learn

DATE PALM.

that every kind of literature, save the dramatic, was composed by them. Astronomy, philosophy, religion, architecture, sculpture, painting, imposing rituals for the dead, a learned priesthood and elaborate systems of theology, society, and government then flourished in the valley of the Nile, and prove the existence of a still earlier civilization, of which we know, and shall probably continue to know, absolutely nothing.

* The famous archæologist, Maspero, recently said: " Egypt is far from being exhausted. Its soil contains enough to occupy twenty centuries of workers; for what has come to light is comparatively nothing."

Close by the temple is the Sphinx itself, crouching in silence by the sea of sand, as if to guard the royal mausoleums. This monster, whose human head and lion's body typified a union of intelligence and strength, was hewn out of the natural rock on the edge of the desert, and only in places

SPHINX AND PYRAMID.

where the stone could not adapt itself to the desired form was it pieced out with masonry. From the crown of its head to the paved platform on which rest its outspread paws, it measures sixty-four feet. The sand has long since encroached upon this space, but formerly it was kept free from all incursions of the desert, and between its huge limbs stood an altar dedicated to the Rising Sun, before which must have knelt unnumbered thousands of adoring worshipers.

To-day the Sphinx appears as calm and imperturbable as it did six thousand years ago. It is probably the oldest relic of human workmanship that the world knows—the silent witness of the greatest fortunes and the greatest calamities of time. Its eyes, wide open and fixed, have gazed dreamily out over the drifting sands, while empires, dynasties, religions, and entire races have risen and passed away. If its stony lips could speak, they might truthfully utter the words " Before Abraham was, I am." It was, indeed, probably two thousand years old when Abraham was born.

It is the antiquity of the Sphinx which thrills us as we look upon it, for in itself it has no charms. The desert's waves have risen to its breast, as if to wrap the monster in a winding-sheet of gold. The face and head have been mutilated by Moslem fanatics. The mouth, the beauty of whose lips was once admired, is now expressionless. Yet grand in its loneliness,—veiled in the mystery of unnumbered ages,— this relic of Egyptian antiquity stands solemn and silent in the presence of the awful desert — symbol of eternity. Here it disputes with Time the empire of the past; forever gazing on and on into a future which will still be distant when we, like all who have preceded us and looked upon its face, have lived our little lives and disappeared.

O sleepless Sphinx!
Thy sadly patient eyes,
Thus mutely gazing o'er the shifting sands,
Have watched earth's countless dynasties arise,
Stalk forth like spectres waving gory hands,
Then fade away with scarce a lasting trace
To mark the secret of their dwelling-place:
O sleepless Sphinx!

EGYPT

O changeless Sphinx!
In the fair dawn of time
So grandly sculptured from the living rock;
Still bears thy face its primal look sublime,
Surviving all the hoary ages' shock;
Still art thou royal in thy proud repose
As when the sun on tuneful Memnon rose:
O changeless Sphinx!

O voiceless Sphinx!
Thy solemn lips are dumb;
Time's awful secrets hold'st thou in thy breast;
Age follows age,--revering pilgrims come
From every clime to urge the same request,—
That thou wilt speak.   Poor creatures of a day,
In calm disdain thou seest them die away:
O voiceless Sphinx!

Majestic Sphinx!
Thou crouchest by a sea
Whose fawn-hued wavelets clasp thy buried feet;
Whose desert surface, petrified like thee,
Gleams white with sails of many an Arab fleet;
Or when wild storms its waves to fury sweep,
High o'er thy form the tawny billows leap:
Majestic Sphinx!

Eternal Sphinx!
The pyramids are thine;
Their giant summits guard thee night and day;
On thee they look when stars in splendor shine,
Or while around their crests the sunbeams play;
Thine own coëvals, who with thee remain
Colossal genii of the boundless plain:
Eternal Sphinx!

www.ingramcontent.com/pod-product-compliance
Lightning Source LLC
Chambersburg PA
CBHW030539270326
41927CB00008B/1436